LEADERSHIP

BECOME A SUPER LEADER

MANAGEMENT, MANAGEMENT SKILLS, COMMUNICATION & COACHING

J.P. Richardson

© 2015

COPYRIGHT NOTICE

DISCLAIMER

Although the author and publisher have made every effort to ensure that the information in this book was correct at press time, the author and publisher do not assume and hereby disclaim any liability to any party for any loss, damage, or disruption caused by errors or omissions, whether such errors or omissions result from negligence, accident, or any other cause.

TABLE OF CONTENTS

INTRODUCTION

History is littered with examples of great leaders; these are people who inspire others in times of great need and those who motivate others to make the world a better place. Leaders are an essential part of life; whether in business matters or your personal life. They are excellent at communicating their intentions, spotting the potential of specific people and motivating them to get the job done.

However, a leader does more than ensure a job is completed; they are there to offer guidance to others, this will build the confidence of those completing the work and enable them to set their own mini-targets. In effect a good leader will help his followers to develop and become better people.

Of course, not everyone in the world can be a leader. Some people are born with a natural tendency to lead others, whilst many people are simply looking for someone to provide them with safety, nurture and support. There is an essential demand for all types of people; leaders are not necessarily the best people to actually get the job done. They are the ones that can motivate and inspire people with the necessary skills; this is why it is essential to acknowledge every member of a team; because every member makes a job possible.

Many people will be content to follow as this will provide them with the safety and security they desperately want; this is a primeval instinct; a desire to be led and protected. Super leaders recognize the need for followers and will look after their needs. They will also recognize that, at times, their style of leadership will need to change in order to achieve the right result.

The best leaders are those which have an affinity with those they lead; they build a relationship with their followers. This affinity is what allows someone to lead, without it there will always be resistance to the decisions and actions they take. Leaders are also an essential part of everyday life; a leader is essential to provide guidance and direction to others. People who band together without a leader will usually end up arguing amongst themselves and their project will fall into chaos. A leader will resolve conflicts and impose the guidelines necessary to ensure everyone has an opportunity to voice their opinion.

It is important to note that a super leader does not ignore the opinions of their followers; the best leaders will involve their followers and seek their opinions before making a decision which is based upon the best interests of all involved. A leader should also be able to envision the future; whether this is a politically changed future, a business led experience or simply the completion of a dream. It is their vision which inspires others and brings about positive change.

Perhaps the fundamental belief held by all leaders is that they know how to get something done and they take the necessary steps to make it happen.

CHAPTER 1 – THE KEY ATTRIBUTES OF A SUPER LEADER

Most great leaders have natural leadership qualities; however, it is possible to learn how to become a super leader. The first thing which you should establish is whether you already have the key attributes of a super leader or whether you need to develop your skills:

- **Honesty**

This skill is essential in all walks of life but it is especially important if you are the leader. You will need to be honest with your team about what you expect from them, you will need to be honest with yourself about what is possible and you need to be honest with others outside of your project to ensure it is taken seriously and the support needed is given.

Being honest will also ensure that anyone you deal with will respect your wishes and attempt to help you; simply because they will know where they stand and that you are unlikely to double cross them.

- **The ability to delegate**

A great leader will know that it is not possible to do everything themselves. In fact, not only are there not enough hours on the day to do everything you need; there are others who will be much better at doing the job. The best leaders accept their own limitations and use the skills of the people they have on their team to achieve their goals.

Delegating ensures your team will feel involved in the project and this will ensure they remain motivated. It is important for them to know their input makes a difference.

- **Confidence**

Even the best leaders will find there are times when things do not go to plan. This is one of the times it is essential to have confidence in your own actions and the project you are undertaking. There will always be set backs but you must focus on the long term goal. A confidence in your ability to get the right result will ensure you keep going when things get tough. It is this attitude and the confident attitude you project which will ensure your team continue to be inspired and push the project forward; no matter what the obstacles. They will take their lead from you.

- **Dedication**

Just as you need to be confident that your vision can become a reality you also need a dedication to your chosen project. Your level of dedication will be noticed by your team and they will strive to reach the same level of dedication.

This will be of great benefit if you find that you doubt the wisdom of your own tactics; their unquestioning faith in your abilities will inspire you to continue.

An essential part of your dedication is allowing your team to see it. A team which sees you working long hours and prepared to tackle any job will become as dedicated as you are. You can, literally, lead by example.

- **Creativity**

In order to direct other people and lead them to a better future you will need to have a creative streak. It is this creativity that will allow you to find an alternative solution to a problem. In fact, it is this which made the project possible. A super leader only becomes one because they are creative enough to see a new version of the future and focus on how to achieve that vision.

Your creative streak will also allow you to find a solution quickly when faced with a problem or issue. Sometimes it is not possible to complete a task in the traditional manner and you will need to think outside of the box to find a solution which works; with the resources you have to hand.

- **Communication**

This is, possibly, the most important attribute that every leader has to have. You must be able to communicate your wishes and desires effectively; this will ensure your team is aware of what is expected of them.

The best leaders will have mastered communicating effectively and concisely on many different levels; your team will need to know your goals and the work methods you wish to employ to make this a reality. Alongside this, you will need to communicate the guidelines regarding expected behavior, expectations and even provide feedback on their efforts so far.

- **Positive Attitude**

Every super leader needs a positive attitude. There is no problem which cannot be overcome and no issue which cannot be resolved. A positive attitude is essential to ensure you do not fall at the first hurdle. There will be obstacles and challenges along the way and you will need to overcome these.

A positive attitude will also be seen by your team and your own, upbeat approach, will start to influence them; they will adopt the same attitude. If the majority of your team have a positive, can-do attitude then anything is possible!

A positive attitude can also help you and your team to get over any internal issues or mistakes; instead of dwelling on them a good leader should learn from them and move on; always focus on the positive and the future.

- **Sensitive Approach**

You must be sensitive to the needs of those around you, the global economy and even any competition. Sensitivity is often seen as a weakness; however, it is actually a distinct advantage to a leader.

Allowing your sensitivity to come through will enable you to be aware of what is happening around you.

This may be personal problems that some of your team are having or an issue in the market which is just developing. Sensitive people tend to be more in-tune with the environment around them; if you improve your sensitivity you are more likely to see issues before they arise.

- **Inspirational**

A super leader is seen as inspirational; this means they are able to visualize a concept in the future and make it a reality. In fact, you can be inspirational in a much more down to earth fashion. Share your vision and your passion for the vision with your team; this will motivate and inspire them to believe in your dream.

Your inspiration can become the dream for many people if you focus on both the end result and inspiring those around you to achieve it. This will enable you to build something for the future which can, potentially, inspire millions of people and it will ensure your team has a reason to work hard and succeed.

- **Intuitive**

Intuition is often referred to as your gut feeling; it is about being aware of everything which is going on around you and relying on your own instincts to tell you what is going to happen next. The market place and the global economy are constantly changing and you may need to react quickly to a new development.

As already mentioned, this may mean thinking out of the box and coming up with a unique solution; part of being able to do this is using your intuition and basing your decision in this. A good leader will spend time contemplating all the relevant issues to ensure they have the best possible solution and then implement it.

If your intuition tells you a previous decision may have been wrong then do not dwell on it, simply learn and move forward.

- **Decisive**

When a decision does need to be made a great leader will look at all the relevant information and base their decision on the evidence in front of them. This is an important attribute which you must develop; gather as many facts together as you can and then decide what you believe the best approach to be. Once you have made a decision stick to it and move forward.

It is important to note that sometimes you will need to make a decision on the spot and other times you will have time to consider the facts in detail. To ensure you are able to make a decision you should keep abreast of all updates and changes to both your project and anything which may affect it. This will ensure you can make the best decision possible and make the decision quickly when necessary.

Being able to make quick, fair decisions will also inspire confidence in your team; if they believe you are in control and know what you are doing they will respond well to your demands.

- ## The Ability to Listen

This is an essential skill in any walk of life; it is also one that every leader should practice and work to become excellent at. The best negotiations and conversations are had when you spend at least eighty percent of the time listening to the other person.

Listening allows you to find out what issues are occurring; whether personally with your staff or in connection with the project. If you know what the issue is you will be able to react and deal with it appropriately; this is simply not possible without listening!

The best leaders will be willing to listen to others as their ideas may even improve the ultimate vision; this is often true when people who are working on a particular part of the project. They are likely to have an in-depth knowledge of one item and how it affects the whole or how it can run better.

Listening also allows your team to know that their opinion counts; this will make them feel valued and will ensure they work harder and are more committed to the project.

- ## Responsibility

A super leader recognizes that they have a responsibility to themselves, to their team and to the goal of their project. At all times, a leader needs to be aware of the needs of their team and their project; they must also be prepared to take responsibility for the actions of their team. Leaders need to understand

and acknowledge that the success or failure of any project is governed by their leadership, innovation and motivation to succeed. The responsibility will fall on your shoulders; even if it is a member of your team that causes the project to fail.

The reason behind this is that a leader is supposed to motivate and ensure the project is completed successfully; you have to be willing to do whatever it takes to ensure your project succeeds, to make it happen. It is this quality which will allow you to lead others to a successful result; their success is your success and their failure is also shared.

- **Sense of Humor**

It can be very easy for a project to take over your life and for you to obsess about the result or direction in which the project is going. However, a truly great leader will recognize that the best work is produced by people who are relaxed and enjoying their work. It is, therefore, your responsibility to ensure that people are given the opportunity to relax and unwind. The more complex the project or the more pressing the deadline; the more important this becomes. Having a sense of humor will allow you to connect directly with your team and build relationships with them.

It can also be used to lighten the mood and show that you are human. This will help others to trust you as you are showing that you are both human and approachable. This relaxes people and will allow their creative side to emerge and provide new ways of solving issues or moving a project forward.

Optimistic

A leader needs to be optimistic; you need to be able to focus on the good in any situation and use this to inspire your team and you. This will ensure you are always moving forward and that you team are comfortable coming to you to solve a problem.

Being optimistic will also allow you to see the potential in two, or more, people working together and the results which can be achieved. Your optimism will inspire others to achieve more and do what they may have thought was impossible.

Perhaps most importantly, it will ensure you always believe there is a way forward; this belief will filter down to your team and, together, you will be able to find the right path.

CHAPTER 2 – BUILDING YOUR MANAGEMENT SKILLS

An important part of being a super leader is understanding how to manage people; their expectations and the best method to ensuring they consistently provide their best effort. To ensure you get the most out of your team and drive your project forward it is essential to understand and build upon these management traits:

- **Giving Feedback**

Your team is made up of people and the majority of people like to have feedback, whether positive or negative. As a good leader you should make time to speak regularly to each member of your team and provide them with this feedback. This will help to motivate and inspire them; it will also provide you with the opportunity to ensure things are being done correctly.

Feedback can be given at any time; you should not wait for a review. This is particularly true if you become aware of an issue which needs resolving; there is no sense in waiting for someone's next review.

Out of respect for your staff you should only provide your constructive feedback in private to the team member concerned. Embarrassing them in front of the rest of the team will not help team morale or productivity. If you need to praise a team member this can be done publicly as it is good for others to be aware of how someone has helped the team and the fact that it has been noted.

- **Make Time for your Team**

Your team is made up of people, each one of them has their own problems and issues to face and they may need your support. It is essential to make time for your team by blocking off a little piece of time every day in which you can talk to some or all of them and establish if they have any issues which they need help with; at work or home.

Alongside this it is essential for your team to know that you are always available to discuss their needs and issues. This does not mean that they can disturb you at any time of the day; but they should be aware that if they let you know they need to talk you will find time for them.

Remember; your team is your most important asset!

- **Balance**

There must be a balance between being too friendly and not being approachable; you will also need to be a part of every detail of the project without micro managing it. Your team should be able to complete the tasks assigned to them without you watching their every move; however you do need to monitor their progress to ensure a project is being completed on time and in the manner expected. It is of little benefit to discover at the end of a project that one part has been completely misconstrued!

Learning to find the right balance will leave your team free to be creative and flourish without damaging the project.

- **Friendship**

The smaller the team you operate the easier and potentially more tempting it will be to befriend your colleagues. However, as a super leader this is not a good idea! Managers who are too friendly with their staff will generally blur the line between friendship and professionalism. This will often result in an abuse of the relationship by one or both sides as the need to look after a friend overrides the needs of the project.

Being too friendly with your team will also make it extremely difficult to be fair, or even make a decision if tough action has to be taken. This is not to say that you cannot socialize and enjoy time with your team; but it must be done in moderation.

- **Motivating**

A great leader recognizes that every member of their team needs to be motivated. One of the most common mistakes is assuming that motivation stems from an increased financial reward. However, there are many different ways to motivate your team and you need to understand the priorities and desires which govern each if your staff. Some of your team may prefer to be able to work remotely, whilst others might like the idea of flexi-time.

As a manager and a leader you need to establish what it is that each of your team values most; you can then offer this as both an incentive and a reward.

- **Recruiting**

There are a variety of times when you will need to recruit a new member of staff for your team. This may be to replace a member, or to add members to your team. This can often be a rushed process as you attempt to deal with hundreds of application forms and allow time to conduct interviews. The result of this is that the selection process is often rushed and you do not, necessarily pick the best person.

It is essential to put enough time aside to do this properly; you will need to think about the position which they are fulfilling and what qualities they need. You must also think about whom they will be working with and how well they will integrate with your existing team.

Finally, taking the time to pick the right candidate will mean that your training time should be minimal and you will not need to repeat the whole process in a few weeks when they quit.

- **Being a Role Model**

The best leaders will set an example by how they approach the daily challenges and their dedication to the job in hand. A good leader will refrain from making negative comments, particularly about any other member of the team. If you do make negative comments you will find it difficult to tell your staff not to do the same. Having a negative attitude and approach to any part of the project, or any individual involved will lead to negative vibes and a general reduction in morale. This will affect productivity and creativity.

- **Delegating Responsibility**

A good manager knows he cannot control or physically do anything. In fact, the best managers do not even need to be present for their teams to know what to do and how to get on with the project. The best managers consolidate all the information available and assign jobs to their team based upon each person's skill set.

Part of this is also learning to delegate the responsibility. Although you will be responsible for the job as a whole, there is no reason why your team cannot deal with many of the day to day issues and handle their own part of the responsibility. This can be backed up by a relevant reward system.

Passing in responsibility for parts of the job will ensure you remain free to manage the project as a whole and do not get bogged down in the detail.

- **Know Your Team**

A good manager knows what each of their team is capable of and utilizes these skills to aid the team. This may mean acknowledging that someone is better than you at doing a particular task; and allowing them to do the necessary work.

Knowing your team will also allow you to be aware of any issues as they arise and, if necessary ensure certain people work on different parts of the project to prevent personalities clashing. It is inevitable that some people will not get along with each other and part of your job as a manager; is to know these issues and creating a work environment which will stimulate every member of your team.

By knowing your team and delegating responsibility to them, you will improve productivity and morale.

- **Constructive Criticism**

A necessary factor of being a super leader and a manager of people is that there are times when you will need to correct their actions and even adjust their method of working. This needs to be done promptly. The longer someone is left to adopt an incorrect or bad procedure the more difficult it will be to stop them doing it in the future and the more damage they are likely to inadvertently do to the project.

Constructive criticism should be offered in a private environment where other members of the team cannot hear what is being said. This will help to prevent embarrassment and any ill-feeling. It will also provide you with an opportunity to assess your staff member and confirm they are happy within their role.

- **Opportunities For Improvement**

Many people work better when they can see that, not only is the project going somewhere, but that there are opportunities for them to rise through the ranks and take on more. This will not appeal to every member of your team but it will be important to some.

To promote this feeling it is essential to promote from within your team, whenever possible. You also consider ways in which you can reward staff for jobs well done, in particular for taking on extra duties. This will ensure your team feel appreciated and know that there are future prospects if they want them.

- **Goals**

The project goal should be to complete the given assignment and provide a product or service which does exactly what you set out to achieve. However, this can be a big, long term goal and it can be difficult for people to feel truly motivated and inspired about a goal that is some distance in the future.

To successfully lead and inspire your team you should break the project into as many small goals as possible and aim for one goal at a time with your team. This will also help to provide a timescale for the ultimate goal and keep your project on track.

Every mini-goal achieved should be celebrated with the team; this will ensure they remain motivated and focused.

- **Negotiation**

Even if you are the best manager in the world you cannot be right all the time. The bigger your project, dream or business; the more essential it is to have other people dealing with the day to day activities. As already discussed, it is essential for you to utilize your skills and seek the assistance of others to deal with the items you are not so good at.

However, every time you introduce new people to your project you will also have an abundance of new ideas and opinions. To be a super leader you must develop the skill of negotiation; you will need to keep all members of your team as happy as possible and keep the project heading in the right direction!

Perhaps the most important aspect of this key management trait is to be able to listen to all parties and sides of any arguments. Understanding what your team, or even a competitor needs, will enable you to find a solution which suits everyone. There is always a middle ground and the art of negotiation is finding that ground and making the most of every opportunity. You may even be surprised at the ideas which evolve from your team and how they can propel your project onwards.

- **Recognize Achievements**

Everyone likes to feel that they are working for a reason and that they are not just a cog in the team. One of the easiest ways to achieve this is to recognize any achievement; no matter how big or small. The recognition can be public or private; this should depend upon your knowledge of the individual and the appropriate reward for the accomplishment.

It is important to note that recognition does not have to be financial, although the majority of people will accept a monetary reward, they will also accept many other gestures; such as a day out, vouchers for an evening meal at a nice restaurant. It is often not the gift that is it important, it is the recognition.

This is also an excellent way to motivate your team and ensure they feel like part of your project; this will inspire them to be more productive, innovative and loyal. Each of these characteristics will help you to focus on the project and what matters; not expending valuable time and effort dealing with the mundane issues.

- **Structure**

For any manager to succeed in both managing and directing a team it is essential to both have a structure in place and for everyone to know and understand this structure. You may wish to discuss this with your team before creating it or you may already have it in place from the very beginning.

A structure will allow every member of your team to understand their role and who they need to report to; it will ensure that all matters are dealt with fairly and efficiently. It will also allow you to define who is responsible for every section of the project of the business and simplify the reporting process. This will ensure you have the right information available when required and are able to focus on what matters.

- **Values**

Without your team you will not be able to complete your project or reach the goals you have set yourself. The first part of this quality is ensuring that you have your own set of values and that you live by these values. These should be the same values that you expect your staff to work by; they will be able to see that you also adhere to these values and lead by example.

The second part of this essential quality; is the ability to value the contribution of others. This will produce their best efforts and will allow you to help them develop personally and professionally. Encouraging personal development; is an essential way of showing your team that you value them, and their contribution.

A further way of showing that you value your team is to ensure you remain flexible and approachable for your team. No matter how great their commitment to you and your project they will, at times, have family issues which should take precedent over anything else. It is important to be flexible and as accommodating as possible to show how much you value each of your team.

- **Priorities**

It is also essential to be able to prioritize your workload, your goals and your team. This should involve creating a plan everyday and building in the flexibility to adjust your schedule to fit any new events or occurrences.

Understanding your priorities will ensure you focus on one thing at a time. This is an essential tactic to getting something done; you will achieve significantly more by tackling one job after another and dedicating one hundred percent of your efforts into the task in hand.

Understanding which job needs to be done when will also show your team that you are a positive, decisive leader; you will inspire them.

CHAPTER 3 - LEARNING TO COMMUNICATE EFFECTIVELY

Communication is essential to being successful both in business and in your personal life. It is something that everyone does on a daily basis; it may be as simple as greeting a colleague or friend, alternatively it could be presenting a project to a group of investors or even making a public speech. Whatever the event, being able to communicate effectively and win your audience over is the one of the most important skills in becoming a super leader.

The following techniques will help you to become the best communicator possible:

- **Personal Conversations**

In order for your conversation to appeal, it must be targeted at a personal level. Whether you are talking to one person or a hundred; you must allow the audience to hear and see you as a person. The best way of doing this is to introduce a short anecdote of your own; one that shows your struggle to survive against great adversity and the way you triumphed. This will show those who are listening, that you are a real person; just as you have the ability to empathize with your audience, they will be able to empathize with you.

This will make it much easier to communicate your ideas and gain support when required.

- **Target your Audience**

No matter what size your audience is it is essential to understand what they would like to gain from a conversation. This will allow you to deal with their issue first and ensue they understand; not only do you know what they need but that you are in a position to give them that something; providing they meet you halfway.

Knowing what someone is after can be a great benefit in any conversation; it is also extremely useful when negotiating with suppliers, customers or even competitors.

The best leaders know how to communicate their needs to others and inspire them with their own vision. This is a result of knowing your audience and what they need; whilst speaking to them on a personal level.

- **Understand your Body Language**

Your body can say a huge amount about your attitude, perspective and even your mood. It is essential to study your own body movements; one of the most obvious is the inability to stay still. This is usually a sign of nervousness although it can be seen as being passionate about a subject. Crossing your arms across your chest is a defensive stance and suggests someone who will be disagreeable and stubborn; not a desirable trait when attempting to communicate with someone!

If you are unsure about the message your body language is giving out then you should replay a conversation or speech in front of your mirror; once you are alone. You may be surprised at the way your body talks; being aware of this will make it much easier to negate any negative effects and give off the right message when communicating with people. Communicating well is essential if you wish people to see you as a great leader.

- **Be Direct**

One of the most difficult things to do when discussing an issue with anyone is to be completely honest. There are certainly times when being completely honest can work to your detriment. However, generally it is agreed that the best policy when discussing an issue is to be honest about your concerns or desires and tell the other party exactly what you wish to gain from the meeting.

This will ensure that both parties know and understand your motivation and position. It is then up to them if they wish to work with you. At the very least you are giving them a fair warning that you are after one thing and they may need to decide what is most important to them and their own goals.

- **Listening**

This trait is essential no matter which leadership role you undertake. In fact; it is often the most underrated and useful skill to develop when negotiating with anyone else. Talking is an essential part of communicating and properly listening and absorbing the information is essential.

Listening will do more than allow you to understand the risks and desires of the other party; it will also build trust and respect. Others will see that you take the time to listen and will value that in you as a person; this will make you appear trustworthy and people tend to respond well to trust issues.

- **Open-minded**

Becoming a super leader requires you to be open-minded regarding the opportunities available and whether these ideas come from your team or another source. You should also be open-minded to other avenues of communication; whether this is social media or trailing a banner behind a plane.

The real trick is not in which method you use but it is in understanding the different venues out there and when to choose the relevant one. Open-mindedness is allowing anyone the opportunity to contribute their ideas; regardless of their social standing or even the validity of the idea.

- **Know your Subject**

If you are talking to someone about something, be certain that you know your facts before passing on any information. If you do not know your subject, this may become apparent to anyone who does understand the subject and will ruin your credibility; which should have been well established at this point.

Understanding what you are talking about will enable you to field questions at any time; whether in a pre-arranged place or out of the blue. Being this well prepared at all times will ensure you are ready for the any opportunity which comes your way!

- **Read between the Lines**

It is often the case in both everyday conversations and within a more professional setting that the best information is not what is said but what is not said.

There is a great deal of information which can be tapped into if you know how to listen and understand what is not being said but is being referred to. This skill may sound difficult but it is surprisingly easy to develop. Simply start by concentrating on what the other party are telling you; then compare this with their stated aim and you will see what elements have been left out of the conversation.

You will then be able to introduce these elements in your own terms and make it very difficult for the other party to say no.

- **Flexibility**

Communicating with anyone requires you to be flexible. You must be prepared to change your approach; particularly if new information comes to light which changes the way you view a situation.

All conversations should be allowed to flow freely until a natural resolution appears. Communication, by its very nature, should be flexible and almost impossible to drag in a certain direction. It is also important to note that communication can be completed in many different forms and it is essential to be flexible as to which is the best approach for any given situation.

- **Watch for Misunderstandings**

When discussing any issue or subject with someone it is very easy for the other party to 'get the wrong end of the stick'. The result will probably be obvious as their responses will change. You will be able to monitor for an extremely positive or negative change in their behavior and responses; this will signal that your conversation has gone downhill rapidly.

You should then be able to quickly correct the issue and ensure the conversation remains on track.

- **Never lay Blame**

It is very easy, and understandable, to look for someone to blame when things have not gone according to plan. However, blaming someone creates a bad environment for everyone on the project and is not productive in communicating or resolving an issue. The best way to move your project forward is not to dwell on the mistake but to look at what it is possible to learn and how to improve the communication and response to an issue in the future.

Blaming someone or several someone's will simply detract from the aims of the project and hinder your progress.

- **Social Media**

Not all communication is verbal, or via your body language! Modern technology has brought social media to every person in the world. It is easy to get online and create a profile on any one; or even all, the available social media platforms.

Social Media provides you with the power and the opportunity to reach many thousands of people every day. However, you must consider the message and the image that you are portraying; too serious and you will drive many customers away, whilst too relaxed will not show you in a professional light. Obtaining the right balance can be exceptionally tricky but also provides an opportunity to communicate effectively with many different market segments.

- **Advertising Online**

Another highly productive method of communicating with your customers or potential customers is through online advertising. Online advertising can be as simple as creating pop-up ads which appear when people search on specific subjects or go to certain web pages. It can also be much more involved and include the building of a social media account and creating a group of followers.

Whichever route you choose to take, communicating with customers, other experts in your field, or even investors is a viable, but sometimes difficult option. Social media will leave you open to 'throw-away' comments by others; comments which if not handled correctly can do serious damage to your image and reputation. Again, you will need to manage this form of communication carefully to ensure your projected image is what you want it to be.

- **Email**

One email can be sent to hundreds, or thousands of people. The process can be largely automated; you simply create the message and select the people who you want to send it to. For this to work effectively you need to divide your followers into groups; preferably by interests or age: this will ensure you send relevant information to each follower.

An email is a powerful tool but it is also possible to get it wrong and do serious damage to your profile and your following. It is something else that needs to strike the right balance between professional and friendly; you need to be seen as approachable but you will never be able to individually answer all your followers; it would simply be too time consuming.

- **Never be Afraid of Silence**

When communicating with others; whether one to one or even when giving a speech, it is important to recognize that there will be times when short periods of silence will occur. This is not something to be afraid of!

Silence, during any form of communication allows you to collect your thoughts and keep a conversation on track. It also allows you and your audience an opportunity to absorb the information and formulate an opinion; this will ensure any conversation is meaningful and useful.

In negotiating terms, silence is often an essential ingredient and follows the making of an offer; it is usually the person who breaks the silence first who will yield on the issue. In fact, silence can be a very useful way of communicating any message!

- **Anticipation**

One of the most important skills which must be learnt to ensure effective communication with a wide range of people is the ability to anticipate what the other party needs, wants or is about to ask for. Understanding and anticipating this desire can be achieved by researching and educating yourself in the way that other people do business and how they react in certain situations.

Understanding this will allow you to create the right scenario and assure you of achieving the right result; the majority of your success will be a result of planning and environment; not a result of your actual words.

- **The Importance of Eye Contact**

When communicating with people in person, it is essential to maintain eye contact as much as possible. Of course, too much direct eye contact may seem intimidating and a little over the top. However, get it right and people will automatically trust you as they will believe you are being open and honest. Trust is an integral part of communicating to enable you to build relationships and obtain the desired result when dealing with other parties.

One of the best tricks, in a one to one situation, is to focus on a spot above someone's eyes, anywhere on the forehead. This will ensure you are making eye contact without intimidating them or yourself. A group scenario will involve constantly scanning the group, pausing for a few moments on each person to ensure they feel you are creating a direct connection with them.

- **Practice Speeches**

Public speaking is a necessary, although often terrifying part of communicating with people. It is also a key trait of every great leader and an essential skill to master to ensure you become a super leader.

Nerves tend to be the biggest issue when faced with a public speaking event; the majority of people will worry about if they are liked and their speech is appreciated. However, one of the basic criteria for giving a good public speech is focusing on what your audience is hoping to obtain by listening to your speech. The attention should not be on you or whether you are liked, this is a foregone conclusion if your speech has delivered their expectations.

Public speaking is a very effective way of communicating with many people at the same time. It is a skill which is best mastered by practice. You should practice presenting the information via the use of a few key prompt cards; these should be enough to keep you on track when communicating without simply reading your speech from the paper. The more you practice the easier and more comfortable public speaking will feel.

- **Be True to Your Values**

It is essential to know your own principles and values; and then to live by them. This will help you to become the person you would like to be and to effectively communicate with others. The reason for this is that the more you know yourself, your limits and your values, the more comfortable you will feel in your own skin.

Knowing yourself allows you to focus on delivering the right product and still stick to your chosen values. It is this, indirect form of communication, which will ensure you come across as charismatic and make it much easier for others to want to follow your lead.

- **Recognize the Importance of Different Opinions**

Every member of your team and even your target audience will have a slightly different outlook on life and this will result in a myriad of different opinions. Every one of these opinions is valid and can be an essential part of the development process.

Recognizing the different opinions and learning to communicate with each of them will allow you to make the most of every resource you have available.

Chapter 4 – The Importance of Coaching Others and Learning to Delegate

Coaching others is an essential part of developing and communicating; both as an individual and as a member of a group. A super leader will look to impart the wisdom and knowledge they have gained to ensure others are able to follow in their footsteps and, if necessary, continue what they started. The best leaders will inspire others to undertake a task that they may have though impossible on their own; yet with a little coaching is easily within their skill set.

There are many different aspects of coaching and delegating effectively; used properly these skills can be developed and improved to establish a group of people which will assist you in leading your team and reaching your goals:

- **Understanding the Current Skill set of your Team**

In order to fully appreciate and drive your team forward it is essential to understand them and what motivates them. This is the best way of establishing a good knowledge of their skill set and of which approach is best to obtain results.

Once you understand what your team is capable of you will be able to identify where improvements can be made and the best method for achieving these improvements. This is stage one of coaching, identifying their needs and building on their current abilities; this will ensure your team is constantly challenged and open to new experiences and goals.

In the majority of cases your team will welcome the additional responsibilities and opportunities. Pushing your team to be the best they can be will ensure that they are always providing maximum effort at work. This means that both you and your project will benefit alongside their personal growth.

Understanding your team and their skill set will also ensure that you allocate them jobs within or near their comfort zones whilst gradually coaching them into a new area, or improving their existing skill set.

- **Providing Opportunities to Grow and New Challenges**

The natural follow on from identifying the current skill set of your team is creating the opportunities and challenges for your team. There are many tasks completed daily which can be handled differently and it can be a great learning experience to allow someone, with the right experience and attitude, to tackle these tasks and find their own way of competing the challenge.

The sign of a great leader is being able to entrust these tasks to your staff and being able to guide your team even when they are going in the wrong direction. You must be able to assess how far they can go before they will need correcting and give them as much support as possible along the way. The best leaders do not dictate what to do, but guide others in the right way and allow them to make mistakes and learn from them. A super leader will not judge a mistake made with the right intentions in mind; you should simply see it as an opportunity to grow and try other challenges.

- **Mindfulness**

A great leader must always be mindful of the pressure that is being upon their team. But mindfulness is more than just being aware of your team. It is about leading by example, about learning to be compassionate and creating an atmosphere of self-awareness. In many ways you are creating an atmosphere which allows every member of your team to develop their own mindfulness for others. If every member of your team is looking after each other you will have successfully gained a tight knit, committed team who will be ready and willing to undertake any challenge.

Being mindful is having an awareness of the here and now, despite the need for plans, goals and dreams; it is important to spend some time simply existing in the current moment. Creating this atmosphere in your team allows every one of them to lower their stress levels and become more self-aware; this will allow you and your team to become more aware of your own flaws and the best way to work with them.

Understanding these factors will allow you to have a greater clarity and focus in all that you do.

- **Focusing the Brain**

Coaching others to be the best they can be is often a thankless task; this is because many people either believe they are already perfect, or, they are simply not interested in improving themselves or their life. One of the main aims of any coaching session is to allow your team an opportunity to step back from the pressures of the job and focus their brains on the day to day things. It is essential to focus on each part of the day and look at what you could have learnt.

This attention to detail will force the brain to focus on one thing at a time and you may find there are suggestions and ideas which simply pop into your head. This is a good sign that the coaching is working as you are allowing your own creativity and inspiration to work their magic.

- **Awareness of Opportunities**

To ensure you get the most out of any team; both for yourself and the sake of the team; you need to be aware of any opportunity which could present itself to you. In fact, the idea that anything can be seen as an opportunity should be a basic principle of your team's development. The people who deal with the day to day processes will usually be the ones who see the most opportunities; whether this is to save money or focus on a new direction.

Your team needs to develop an awareness of the world around them and how the general public reacts to the ideas and aspirations that the business believes in. This will help to focus your mind on what works and what does not; which means future projects can be more effectively prioritized and started, according to current trends.

- **Moving the Goal Posts**

Part of coaching a team and being a great leader is to inspire your supporters, but also to remind them that nothing is static, every goal moves depending upon outside influences and the changing perspectives of you and your team. It is important that all members of your team develop an understanding of not just the goals you are all aiming for, but also, of the underlying principles to these goals. This will ensure they are able to react to any changes and suggest ways of improving or modifying the goals to achieve better results.

By coaching your team into the practice of watching and evaluating the goals you will take a huge amount of pressure off yourself and can enjoy focusing on the project development and the overall aim.

You can also ensure that all your team understand that there is no such thing as static in business or life, something is always changing and you must learn to move with it and make the most of every opportunity.

A secondary part of this skill is to teach your team the value of setting their own goals and regularly evaluating them. The best leaders and coaches will encourage their team members to reach and exceed any goal.

- **Understanding the Basic Principles of Leadership**

Perhaps one of the most important skills that any leader should pass on to their team and those around them is an understanding of the principles behind leadership. A great leader is required to be fair, understanding and help to guide their followers along life's journey. Despite the number of challenges that will be faced by any great leader you will also need to be prepared to focus on your team and help them to reach their own goals; even if the only reward you receive is their gratitude.

Leading others means setting an example for others to follow and accepting that this will not always be easy and others will not always be able to follow as they would like to. However, the mark of a great leader is in the optimism and belief they convey; that everyone has the ability to do great things and, with a little help and guidance wants to do so.

Of course, if someone simply requires instructions they can also be a valued member of the team; a good leader understands the strengths and weaknesses of every member of their team and plans the way forward accordingly.

Coaching your team in the roles and principles of leadership will help them to understand your role and how they can become better leaders themselves.

- **Learning to Communicate**

As already discussed, communication is one of the most important traits of any super leader. It is also essential to coach others into this way of thinking and ensure that your entire team understands the power of communication. There are many different methods of communicating with others; they range from simple conversations, boardroom meetings, to emails or customer facing service. The most important principle to be relayed is that every piece of communication should be conducted in a positive manner. Being positive is essential to building a relationship with the other party and obtaining a mutually satisfactory result.

The same principle applies to all levels of communication and it is important to build an understanding of the visual signals that the body gives off when people are discussing things which are important to them. Spotting these signals will enable you to connect with the other party and get the result you need or want. Listening to everything which is said is an important part of communicating and an essential lesson to teach your own team.

The more the team emulates your own standards and behavior the more aware you will become that they have adopted the right approach to communication and others.

- **Coaching as a Source of Information**

Teaching your knowledge and techniques to others is an excellent way of passing on this information to ensure it is available for future generations and to ensure you are building leaders of the future. These leaders may exceed your own skills and capabilities and go much further than even you can dream off! However, coaching them with the necessary skills to become great leaders in their own right also provides an opportunity for you to connect with your team on a personal level and understand them, how they work, how they live and a whole host of other, useful information. The more you understand about your team the easier it will be to both coach them and help them to grow, as people.

It is important to teach your team how to handle and interpret information; they may struggle to see more than one point of view and you can help them to see other viewpoints by asking the right questions. Pushing decisions onto these team members will also ensure that become aware of the responsibility that they hold and that they are allowed to make certain decisions. This will create a feeling of self-worth in your team and encourage them to take on more responsibility and become more dedicated to the team.

- **The Art of Delegation**

Many managers' micro-manage and are extremely reluctant to hand over any control to other members of the team. This can stem from a belief that no one else can do a job as well as you or it can be out of fear that the more which is delegated the less you will be needed. In fact, the best leaders learn to delegate all the time. If there is physically no work left to do then you have done a good job of training all your staff to take care of the everyday items and this will leave you free to focus on keeping your staff happy and ensuring the project or business is moving in the right direction.

The bigger the project or business becomes the more important it becomes to delegate as many roles and tasks as possible; it will simply not be possible to undertake everything yourself and stay focused on your goals, progress and team satisfaction.

The best leaders will pick the tasks they are most suited to and pass the others onto appropriate individuals whilst providing any training which is necessary to ensure they have the skills available to complete the tasks required of them. This is more than just delegation; it is a combination of all the coaching skills, as your team becomes capable of running the project and moving things in the right direction; whether you are there or not. In many ways the ultimate aim of any coaching session is to ensure that a team can survive without your presence.

Despite the importance of being able to delegate it is often one of the most difficult attributes to both teach yourself and coach others in. The following techniques may help you to become better at delegating:

Evaluate the tasks which take up your time during the average week. Consider how much time they take and what skill level is required to so the job properly. Then think about what else you could be doing with that time. You will realize that the time can be far more productively spent and this should convince you to delegate this task to a member of your team. The most difficult part may be deciding which team member should be entrusted with this task.

Instruct your chosen team member carefully, you must be certain that they fully understand what is expected of them and that they will continue to do the job as you have done it. You should be open to the idea of them changing the method, providing the results are still accurate and within the parameters given. However, no employee should change a system without having first used it for an appropriate amount of time; this will ensure they understand all the ramifications of changing it.

One task should be delegated at a time. This will help you to feel more comfortable about someone else doing one of your tasks and will allow you to keep a close eye on the results. As the first task is shown to be completed successfully then you can start to plan the next item to delegate; gradually the pace of delegation will increase as you hand over all the daily tasks, and you will find yourself as busy as ever. The key to delegating successfully is ensuring that the chosen team member understands fully what is expected from them and works towards the same goal as you and the rest if the team.

Delegating anything is probably not a skill which many business owners have in abundance. However, it is an essential skill to master and will allow you to focus on the things that are relevant to your project.

CHAPTER 5 – MOTIVATING YOURSELF AND THOSE AROUND YOU

When you first undertake a project it is very easy to be motivated and push hard to achieve success and get the project off the ground. Unfortunately, once the project is underway it can often be difficult to keep the momentum going; they will be many more demands on your time and a variety of issues which need resolving; possibly even personnel issues. Every drain on your time will make it harder for you to focus on the end goal and may leave you procrastinating at every opportunity you get.

There are several essential tips which you need to follow to ensure you remain motivated and are able to motivate your team:

- Mini Targets

It can be very difficult to aim for a huge goal which may or may not work and is only a possibility at some point in the future. In order to stay motivated and avoid stagnating; it is best to break your project into small pieces and set yourself a host of achievable mini-targets.

These targets should be kept small; ideally they should be achievable within a week and you should provide yourself with a reward every time you reach the target. This will ensure that you take a small step every week and keep your project on track.

The small targets should gradually get bigger so as to ensure everyone is aware of where the project is going and where it may end up.

- The Game

Another good approach is to make the project a game; this is usually an effective way of making sure you not only hit your targets but do more than you need to. The easiest game is to set yourself a simple goal; such as working later every day than you normally do, or even coming in earlier.

You can even up the ante slightly by trying to complete specific tasks in less time than you have done previously; but still to the right standard.

Another version of the game is to complete a specific task in a different way to normal, without affecting the outcome and ensuring that it takes no longer than the usual path would have taken. This can certainly get the brain thinking as you need to understand exactly how something is completed in order to arrive at an alternative solution.

- Deadline

One of the most effective ways to improve the amount of work being produced and ensure that you do not delay is to visualize your working day as the last possible chance to finish a specific project. Working as though you have a deadline will create the pressured environment that many people feel comfortable in; even if it is a more stressful working environment than the normal scenario you are used to.

This is not something that is recommenced every day; not only will it increase the amount of stress you are under, it is also possible it will decrease the quality of the goods you are producing.

It can be a very effective tool when being used to motivate you to achieve your goal.

- Positive Attitude

This trait is as essential as a 'can-do' attitude. No matter how bad it gets you must always look for the silver lining and find something to focus on. This can help to motivate you as you will feel positive about the future. This small amount of positivity will be enough to keep you pushing towards the ultimate goal and will help you to keep the project on track.

A positive attitude will also rub off with the other people involved in the project and the culmination of this will help to drive the project forward as people feel good about the project and their involvement in it.

The power of the positive attitude should never be underestimated. If people feel good then they will always feel more capable and achieve more, no matter what the situation.

- Distractions

One of the biggest reasons why a project does not continue as per the designed schedule is the level of distractions which exist at all times around you and the things you are doing. Absolutely anything can be a distraction; whether someone is riding a unicycle or simply showing a video regarding fishing!

The biggest distractions are the mundane items in your office, your coffee mug, or a blank internet page. The internet can be searched and your coffee mug cleaned, the list of things which suddenly seem important to look at can grow rapidly and take your attention away from the task in hand. No matter how good your intentions, there will be something that can distract you.

The safest route is to remove all the items which can potentially distract you and attempt to focus on the project. Whilst this is a good place to start, it may still be difficult to actually achieve. It may be a better tactic to study the task you need to complete and break it in smaller goals, this may improve your motivation for each task as each one will be easier to achieve and quicker.

- Working Hard

One of the biggest problems with many projects is the sheer size of the project. The simplest way to adjust this is to break each part of the job into different tasks and tackle each task. However, even this more stimulating approach can succumb to a lack of motivation. Instead of focusing on a small section of the plan, you may find it more beneficial to break the plan into small, bite sized chunks and motivate yourself by undertaking one section of the project at a time.

It is far easier to be motivated to do something which can be completed in one day than it is to commit to a much longer term goal. You will gain a sense of satisfaction every day that you have reached your target and that will assist you with completing the entire project.

- Have a Purpose

In order to truly complete the project and stay motivated you will need to define the purpose of the project and remind yourself of it regularly. You may wish to add a relevant picture or postcard which will help you to remember why you are undertaking such a project and how close you are getting to the end result.

Most people take on projects which are close to their hearts and this makes it easier to be passionate about your project. But even if your project relates to something you are truly passionate about, you will need to remind yourself regularly of your purpose; this will ensure you stay on track and deliver the finished project in time.

- Take it Outside your comfort zone

Everyone has a comfort zone, the things they do on a daily basis which they are happy to do; they are known and can even be part of a daily ritual. The longer you spend on a project the more your comfort zone will expand and the less motivated you will become. This will generally mean a more relaxed approach to the project and the slowing down of the expected completion date.

In order to stay motivated and focused it is essential to challenge yourself daily. The best way of doing this is to challenge yourself to do something outside of your normal comfort zone. This task should be tied in to the completion of a daily task, or mini-goal; making the challenge a useful way of staying focused as well a broadening your horizons.

This willingness to try new things will not only help to keep you motivated it should also inspire your team to try the same challenge and they will remain motivated because of your actions.

- Passion

You almost certainly started a specific project because you had an interest in the subject, or a desire to promote it to other people. It is essential to keep this passion alive whilst working on the project. This should not be difficult if you are passionate about the subject. Should you feel your passion starting to wane then you will need to remind yourself about why you love the subject.

It is essential to let your passion show, you should let people know that you are excited by the subject and enjoy what you are doing. Other people will respond to this and be more enthusiastic about the topic; they will also become eager to see what can be achieved and for the project to be a success. This is another way of leading by example; simply allow others to see your passion and they will respond positively.

- Learn Every Day

One of the most important lessons that you should acknowledge is that you do not know it all. There is always scope to learn more and every day brings a new set of challenges which can be dealt with in a new and different way.

Your team will recognize that you are open to new ideas and opinions and will not be afraid to voice theirs. This should lead to frank and open discussions regarding the way forward and all participants will be able to learn from this.

Learning something new every day will ensure you remain passionate about your project and will motivate you to keep looking for new techniques and methods. This approach will show to your team and imbue them with the desire to follow you. Humility is actually an important leadership principle.

- Never Give Up

There will always be times when things go wrong and it may seem impossible to continue. But the sign of a good leader and someone who is personally motivated is when you are not prepared to give up. This does not mean stubbornly remaining on the same track when it is clearly not working! It means making yourself aware of all the options and all the avenues for assistance and using them all to find a way forward.

Having a dedication to your project and picturing the end result will help to inspire you to continue. You may even find it useful to have a personal mantra which sums up why you want a specific project to work. This mantra could be carried with you or displayed in several key places; it will serve to remind and motivate you.

If you show a determination to find a way forward then others will naturally follow you and partake in your desire. They will believe it is possible simply because you do; and that will open up many doors!

- Treat Yourself

In order to stay motivated and continue to motivate your followers it is essential to treat yourself occasionally. If you become obsessed with the project you will quickly stagnate and find yourself stuck in a rut; without being able to see a clear way forward.

Every small achievement should be rewarded, as well as the larger ones, but, more importantly, you should seek to have a small treat every week, ideally this should be time away from your project doing something else that you love. You may want to put all your effort into the project but you will be surprised how much easier it is when you have a little fresh perspective every week. It will help to focus your mind and allow you to see all the options; it will also refresh you and help you to stay enthusiastic and motivated.

Conclusion

Becoming a great or super leader is not something you can do over night; it is not something you are born to do; in fact, the greatest leaders do not see themselves as super leaders at all! This is because a truly super leader will constantly seek to improve their leadership skills and learn more about how they can help their followers. A super leader will recognize that others follow them out of their own choice and can never be forced to follow someone with their heart. A super leader has humility and respects the input and potential that others can add to any project. They are also keen to show their enthusiasm and energy; knowing that it will make others feel the same way.

The best leaders become so over a period of time, they acknowledge that they can and will make mistakes, and they are prepared to learn from them and move forward. This book will have provided you with a guide as to how you can improve your leadership skills and which traits are most desirable.

It is essential to understand that there are key attributes that every super leader must develop and display to ensure others will want to follow them and assist with their projects. Every management skill can be learnt and should be constantly improved on to ensure you are the best manager possible. The better you become at managing people the more you will be in-tune with their hopes and desires and how to motivate them to achieve the best possible results for you and them. A genuine interest in your team and their personal development is essential to becoming a truly super leader.

The book should also have illustrated to you the importance of communicating effectively and that often, this is actually a case of listening first and then thinking before acting or speaking. There are other times when everyone will be waiting for your words of wisdom and you must appear confident and knowledgeable; regardless of how you feel on the inside. Much of the communicating you will do starts with listening and learning from others; this will ensure you have considered all possible viewpoints before you decide which direction to move forward in.

An essential part of this process is guiding and assisting the members of your team in their own personal and professional development. You must be prepared to pass over responsibility to them and allow them to grow as individuals. This will ensure they remain loyal and dedicated to you and your project. Being able to let go and trust your team is an essential skill that you must learn if you are to be a super leader.

Finally, this book will have shown you how important it is to keep yourself and your team motivated, no matter what obstacles come your way. A dedicated, well led team can achieve the seemingly impossible as they will follow you anywhere. If you can inspire this response in people then you are well on your way to becoming a super leader!

Made in the USA
Columbia, SC
08 September 2018